The Thinking Girl's Treasury of Real Princesses

# nur jahan of india

© **2010 Goosebottom Books LLC**
All rights reserved

Series editor **Shirin Yim Bridges**
Consulting editor **Amy Novesky**
Copy editor **Jennifer Fry**
Book design **Jay Mladjenovic**

Typeset mainly in Indonesiana Serif Free and Volkswagen TS
Illustrations rendered in pen and watercolor

Some photographs used under Creative Commons Attribution/Share Alike license
http://creativecommons.org/licenses/by-sa/3.0/

Manufactured in Singapore

Library of Congress PCN 2010903715

First Edition  10  9  8  7  6  5  4  3  2  1

**Goosebottom Books LLC**
710 Portofino Lane, Foster City CA 94404

**www.goosebottombooks.com**

For Tiegan and Alena, the original Thinking Girl
and the real Fairy-Monkey Princess.

~ Shirin Yim Bridges ~


For my family and friends.

~ Albert Nguyen ~

# The Thinking Girl's Treasury of Real Princesses

Hatshepsut of Egypt

Artemisia of Caria

Sorghaghtani of Mongolia

Qutlugh Terkan Khatun of Kirman

Isabella of Castile

Nur Jahan of India

# nur jahan of india

By Shirin Yim Bridges    |    Illustrated by Albert Nguyen

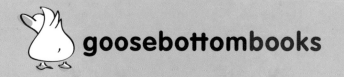

goosebottombooks

# She was called what?!

The foreign words in this book can look strange and hard to pronounce, and dictionaries often don't help — trying to work out dictionary pronunciation symbols can be like trying to read Sanskrit!

Here are most of the unusual names in this book, broken down so that you can say them. (Just don't expect to be understood by an Indian person.)

| | |
|---|---|
| **Nur Jahan** | nur jah•han |
| **Mihr al-Nisa** | meer al•neesa |
| **Jahangir** | jeh•hung•geer |
| **Ladli Begam** | lad•lee bey•gum |
| **Nur Mahal** | nur mah•hal |
| **Asaf Khan** | ah•saf khan |
| **Khurram** | koor•rum |
| **Mumtaz Mahal** | moom•taz mah•hal |
| **Sharyar** | shar•ree•ah |
| **Intimid al-Dawla** | in•tee•mid al•daul•la |

# nur jahan of india

During the time of the Moghul emperors who ruled most of India for over 300 years, no other treasure was as closely guarded as the royal women. In the Moghuls' fairy-tale palaces with their imposing walls, their soaring cupolas and delicate minarets, princesses lived in *purdah*, in complete seclusion from any man outside of their immediate families. They were housed in their own quarters, the *zenana*, which was tucked away in the deepest heart of the palace and approached by a single entrance guarded by eunuchs. (A eunuch is a man who has had his male organs removed so that he can be trusted not to seduce women!) Even the windows of the zenana were screened with elaborate lattice work so that no passing eyes could accidentally fall on a palace beauty.

Yet from behind the screens, without ever breaking purdah, one princess came to rule all of Moghul India. What gave her this power was love. This is a love story — the story of Nur Jahan.

# Where she lived

This map shows the extent of the Moghul Empire when Jahangir inherited it from his father. By the time of Shah Jahan's death (Jahangir's son, the former Prince Khurram), the empire would include all of India except for its southernmost tip.

China

Pakistan

Nepal

Moghul Empire

Arabian Sea

# When she lived

This timeline shows when the other princesses in The Thinking Girl's Treasury of Real Princesses once lived.

| 1500BC | 500BC | 1200AD | 1300AD | 1400AD | 1600AD |
|---|---|---|---|---|---|
| Hatshepsut of Egypt | Artemisia of Caria | Sorghaghtani of Mongolia | Qutlugh Terkan Khatun | Isabella of Castile | Nur Jahan of India |

# her story

Nur Jahan was not born a princess, although she was a distant cousin of the Persian royal family. In fact, she was not born Nur Jahan at all. Her birth name was Mihr al-Nisa (Sun Among Women), and her father was a Persian nobleman who had come to India to work in the Moghul court. It is said that when she was a little girl, she followed her father to work one day and met the future emperor, Jahangir, who was still a boy. Even at that young age, the two fell in love.

▲ You can still visit the Moghul emperors' colonnaded audience hall where Nur Jahan's father would have worked — and where she might have first met the young Jahangir.

Whether or not this story is true, Mihr al-Nisa was married not to the prince but to a diplomat, who took her with him when he was posted to the faraway province of Bengal. (As she was the daughter of a diplomat, this would have been seen as a fitting match. People were very aware of class in those days, and usually married their social equals.) It wasn't until many years later, after her husband had died and Jahangir had become king, that Mihr and her daughter, Ladli Begum, returned to the splendid Moghul court. (You can still see the fabulous Moghul palace that they returned to at the Red Fort in Agra, India.) Mihr joined the palace zenana as the lady-in-waiting to one of Jahangir's stepmothers, and it was in the women's quarters, surrounded by Jahangir's many wives and 300 concubines (official girlfriends or mistresses) that Mihr met Jahangir again.

Mihr al-Nisa had the reputation of being intelligent and beautiful, but she must have been something really special to stand out in that crowd! Even though she was by then 34 years old and considered too old for remarriage by the standards of the day, Jahangir fell head-over-heels in love.

**Oadhani** — head scarf, often beaded, bejeweled, or bordered in elaborate gold embroidery

**Choli** — fitted bodice

**Jewelry** — a part of any Moghul costume, preferably emeralds, rubies, diamonds, and pearls

**Lehenga** — pleated overskirt, frequently made of a muslin so fine that it was transparent

**Pajamas** — loose pants, tighter around the ankles, worn underneath the lehenga; this is where we got the name for clothes comfortable enough to wear to bed!

# What she wore

Nur Jahan was widely credited with having designed fabrics during her reign. Indeed, new textiles appeared that were printed, woven, or embroidered with the same flowers so carefully detailed in her husband's notebooks.

Jahangir was, after all, famous for appreciating all things beautiful. But more than that, he had a great sense of curiosity, a broad range of knowledge, and a sincere passion for the arts. He was a connoisseur (an expert appreciator) of painting and Persian poetry. He kept a journal that you can still read today, in which he recorded his thoughts and findings about everything he saw — including how elephants were born feet first, and descriptions of new flowers and plants that he came across on his journeys. He had a very lively mind. And so did Mihr al-Nisa.

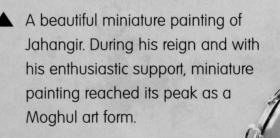

▲ A beautiful miniature painting of Jahangir. During his reign and with his enthusiastic support, miniature painting reached its peak as a Moghul art form.

Detail of another miniature painting, showing the beautiful Nur Jahan.

The beautiful widow was well educated and highly cultivated. (The Persians had an admirable history of educating their women, as you can also see in the book about Qutlugh Terkan Khatun.) She was famous for her good taste and soon influenced court fashions for both men and women. She designed brocades, embroideries, lace, and carpets. She is said to have invented the perfume "attar of roses," the sweet and heavy rose scent still worn by many women around the world. She had a great interest in architecture and designed and commissioned more monuments than Jahangir ever did, monuments that are still considered some of the best examples of Moghul architecture. She was the first to use white marble instead of red sandstone — a trend that would culminate in the Taj Mahal. And above all, she was a poet. She wrote the Persian poetry that Jahangir so loved.

In 1611, within months of their meeting in the zenana, Mihr al-Nisa and Jahangir were married. Jahangir renamed his new wife Nur Mahal, meaning Light of the Palace, and made her his senior wife, whom all the women of the zenana had to obey. (This couldn't have gone down very well in the zenana where, traditionally, the first wife always came first and the most recent wife last. If Jahangir had followed tradition instead of his heart, Nur Mahal would have had no power at all. According to some, Jahangir had as many as 20 wives before her!) The couple spent a lot of time together, and not just the love but the respect between them grew. Jahangir trusted Nur Mahal with the furnishing of the palace and the control of the household finances, and as a result, even as the beauty and magnificence of the Moghul court grew, its running costs decreased. This was entirely due to Nur Mahal's good management.

▲ The zenana at the Moghul palace complex in Agra, where Nur Jahan ruled as Jahangir's senior wife.

With the encouragement of her husband, Nur Mahal began to help Jahangir run not just the court but the country. Royal edicts were signed in both their names, and Jahangir had a gold coin struck with his lovely wife's portrait on the reverse — the first coin to honor a queen in any Muslim country. In recognition of her expanded role in both his life and that of the empire, Jahangir renamed his wife again. No longer was she just Nur Mahal, the Light of the Palace, she was now Nur Jahan, Light of the World.

## What she ate

Nur Jahan was said to have contributed recipes to the flavorful cuisine of the Moghul court. You can still try Moghul food today. Many Indian restaurants use recipes that originated in Moghul imperial kitchens. Moghul cuisine is famous for being rich, creamy, and aromatic. Many ground or whole spices are used, as well as dried fruits and nuts. In addition to the mild Moghul curries, Nur Jahan's husband, Jahangir, was especially fond of the fish known as rohu, and of mangoes and cherries. His favorite non-alcoholic drink was camel's milk.

## Love in white marble

Built on the orders of Nur Jahan, the mausoleum of her father, Intimid al-Dawla, for the first time replaced red sandstone with white marble delicately inlaid with semi-precious stones. This new building style, an expression of Nur Jahan's refined and restrained taste, would become typical of Moghul architecture. Her former ally, Shah Jahan, shared her interest and taste in architecture and brought the use of white marble to its greatest heights in a mausoleum built for his wife — the Taj Mahal. Unequaled in its grace, this monument to a lost love has rightly been called "a teardrop on the cheek of time."

From the zenana, Nur Jahan sent her decisions and directives through her eunuchs to the Emperor and the court, where they were invariably acted upon. Jahangir happily joked that he had given her the country in exchange for some morsels of food and a few cups of wine. The British Ambassador, Sir Thomas Roe, confirmed that Nur Jahan "governs…and wynds him up at her pleasure" — in other words, Nur Jahan had complete control of the Emperor and the empire.

In her work, Nur Jahan was ably supported by her father, and by her brother, Asaf Khan, who soon became the empire's most powerful general. Another ally was Prince Khurram, Jahangir's third and favorite son whom he was openly grooming as heir. In fact, after an introduction by Nur Jahan, Prince Khurram married Nur Jahan's niece, Mumtaz Mahal. (The prince would one day grow up to be Emperor and build for this much-loved wife the wonderful Taj Mahal.)

With her newfound power, Nur Jahan worked on improving trade. In those days, all trade was conducted using long strings (called caravans) of camels. Caravanserais were like motels for these camel trains — or an ancient version of a truck stop. Nur Jahan built caravanserais along all the major trade routes criss-crossing the empire, encouraging trade by making it safe. (The caravanserai she built in Agra could house 2,000 merchants and their camels, with stables for another 500 horses.) The increased taxes that she gained from this growing trade went into the stunning magnificence of the Moghul court, and into the hobbies of her husband. Under Jahangir's generous patronage, a wide range of arts — and Moghul painting in particular — reached its peak.

▲ The caravanserai at Fatehpur Sikri, a Moghul city near Agra where Jahangir was born.

Nur Jahan also worked to improve the lot of women. Although the Moghul court was Muslim, most of India was Hindu, and many families followed the practice of sati, in which a new widow was expected to throw herself onto her husband's funeral pyre. Orders were issued that widows were no longer to be forced to commit suicide. Attempts were also made to put a stop to the practice of killing baby girls. (Sadly, boys were so greatly preferred in India that many families simply killed unwanted girls when they were born.)

But Nur Jahan's life was not all about work. Although she was not supposed to leave the zenana in search of fun, she could bring entertainment inside. One great favorite was the monthly *Mina Bazar*. In the zenana's inner courtyard, fanned by eunuchs and further cooled by fountains, the air sweetened by beds of fragrant flowers, the royal ladies welcomed the Emperor, other men of the royal family, and the wives of the highest nobles. These noblemen's wives brought with them the finest brocades and embroideries, jewels and art objects, turbans and clothes of exquisite finery. (They also brought their daughters, hoping they'd catch the eye of the Emperor or a prince.)

For a few raucous hours, the nobles' wives would conduct themselves as common market traders, offering their wares to the royal family. The Emperor would amuse them all by protesting that the prices were much too high. He would insist on haggling over every penny while the ladies scolded him for not fully appreciating the quality of their goods. After much laughter and merriment, money would change hands and sweets and refreshments would be served. Then, the princesses would disappear into the depths of the zenana until the next Mina Bazar.

Nur Jahan, however, did manage to escape the zenana now and again. She found a way to accompany her husband in one of his favorite pastimes: hunting. Although it might seem offensive to us now, Nur Jahan would go tiger hunting with Jahangir, observing purdah by staying in a closed *howdah* on top of an elephant. All that could be seen of her was the tip of her musket poking through the howdah's drawn curtains. Mounted in this way, she once killed four tigers with six bullets. "Until now," Jahangir wrote proudly, "such shooting has never been seen, that from the top of an elephant and inside of a howdah…six shots should be made and not one miss."

But life did not continue in this idyllic way. Jahangir's health continued to worsen. Nur Jahan found a way to slip away with him to the peace and tranquility of his beloved Kashmir. She nursed him so diligently and tenderly that he sent away the royal physicians, saying that it would be impossible for them to do better. In the face of her husband's approaching death, Nur Jahan now made a great political mistake. She married her daughter, Ladli Begum, to Jahangir's youngest son, Prince Sharyar, and switched her allegiance way from her previous ally, Prince Khurram, to this younger prince.

On October 28th, 1627, Jahangir died. There was a short tussle for the throne, during which Nur Jahan lead an army in person, mounted in a closed howdah on an elephant, and issuing orders through the curtains to a eunuch who passed them on to her officers. (This may be the only time an army has been lead by a woman in purdah!) But there was really no contest. Nur Jahan's own brother, Asaf Khan, India's greatest general and the father of Mumtaz Mahal, was on Prince Khurram's side (after all, the prince was his son-in-law). And Khurram was himself a great military man — and a ruthless one. To ensure there would be no further debate over the succession, he had all his brothers, nephews, and mature male cousins killed.

Nur Jahan got off lightly. She was exiled to Lahore, on a generous pension of 200,000 rupees a year.

# death in exile

Nur Jahan lived another 18 years after the death of her beloved Jahangir. Exiled from the court where she had once had such influence, she spent her time perfecting Jahangir's tomb, planning her own, and writing the Persian poetry that had once enchanted him.

She continued to show concern for the poor, and especially for disadvantaged women. Out of her own funds she provided for the marriages and dowries of more than 500 orphan girls. She also paid for the passage of hundreds of poor who wished to visit the Muslim holy places in Arabia and Persia.

When she died in 1645 of unrecorded causes, the former Prince Khurram, by then Emperor Shah Jahan, allowed her to be buried as she wished. She was laid to rest in an elegant but modest tomb of her own design, in a corner of the garden surrounding the great tomb she had built for Jahangir.

The words on her tomb are her own, and an example of the poetry that Jahangir so loved: "On the grave of this poor stranger, let there be neither lamp nor rose. Let neither butterfly's wing burn nor nightingale sing."